Rising to Purpose
JOURNAL

Rising to Purpose

JOURNAL

A Self-Help Guide To Reach Your Destiny

Shana Danielle

RISING TO PURPOSE JOURNAL

This publication is designed to educate and provide general information regarding the subject matter based on the author's experiences. It is published with the understanding that neither the author nor the publisher is engaged in rendering professional counseling services. Each situation is different, and the advice should be tailored to particular circumstances.

Rising to Purpose Journal- A Self-Help Guide to Reach Your Destiny © 2020 Shana Davis

ALL RIGHTS RESERVED.

This book or parts thereof may not be reproduced in any form, recorded, stored in a retrieval system, or transmitted in any form or by any means, electronic, mechanical, photocopied, recorded or otherwise, without prior written permission from the publisher, except as provided by United States copyright law. For permission requests write to the publisher at: 'Attention Permissions Coordinator' at the address below.

The Shana Danielle Company
227 Market St Suite B.
Camden, NJ 08102

ISBN: 978-1-7353806-2-9

Published by The Shana Danielle Company Camden, NJ

Printed in the United States of America
First Edition September 2020

Cover Design: The Shana Danielle Company
Interior Design: The Shana Danielle Company
Editing: The Shana Danielle Company

Scripture taken from the New King James Version. Copyright 1982 by Thomas Nelson, Inc. Used by permission. All rights reserved.

Scripture quotations marked (NLT) are taken from the Holy Bible, New Living Translation, copyright 1996, 2004, 2015 by Tyndale House Foundation. Used by permission of Tyndale House Publishers, a Division of Tyndale House Ministries, Carol Stream, Illinois 60188. All rights reserved.

Scripture quotations marked (NIV) are taken from the Holy Bible, New International Version, NIV. Copyright 1973, 1978, 1984, 2011 by Biblica, Inc.TM Used by permission of Zondervan. All rights reserved worldwide. www. zondervan.com The ' NIV' and ' New International Version' are trademarks registered in the United States Patent and Trademark Office by Biblica, Inc.TM

Welcome!

Beloved! I am SO glad you are here! This journal was initially created to help me get focused and achieve my goals. Now, I would love to share it with you, in the hope that we can all reach and walk in our purpose.

I am Shana Danielle and I am an inspirational spoken word artist, author, and entrepreneur. I use thought-provoking imagery to encourage and inspire people to become their best, hope-filled, unashamed, unapologetic version of themselves.

I am passionate about helping others to live their best life. God has done amazing things in my life and I know it was not to only enhance me for me, but for me to enhance the kingdom. My family's motto is, " as God blesses us, be a blessing to others" . I am determined to fulfill that calling on my life.

I enjoy meeting new people and helping them identify and achieve their dreams. My motivation comes from a desire to see others succeed, an innate compassion towards others, and a passion to provide exceptional service to all, regardless of background.

My Story...

My book "Rise" - A Collection of Inspirational Poetry, Prose, and Affirmations, was my first step toward providing help for many people seeking to heal from trauma and do better for themselves and their loved ones. This journal is my next step.

While surviving every obstacle that has tried to deter me, I have learned that the past is something that should not define you; however, it can be used as a tool to motivate and encourage others. I have 15 years of experience working with "at-risk youths, substance abuse, and mental health population". My philosophies are faith-based. Fear is not welcomed in my area of expertise. I encourage all to replace fear with faith.

My hope and prayer are that this journal will strengthen and equip you with the tools to reach and walk in your purpose. God has plans to make you prosperous and not harm you. The next few pages will explain how to use this journal. Thank you for allowing me to have a small part in your journey. May God bless you beyond measure!

I love you. It's Time to Rise!

— Shana Danielle

This journal will be...

REFLEXIVE

Each week, it is important to start with what we want to accomplish and focus on. I have provided worksheets in this journal to help you reflect and afterward, rise to walk in your purpose. Every Sunday (or whatever day you choose as the start of your week), you will find a quote for the week and related journal prompt for you to reflect on what you will be working on for each week.

DAILY

Every Monday, you will find a daily journal sheet where I encourage you to start your day with a mantra like "I love the person I am becoming."; write what you are looking forward to today, because it gives you hope, and hope gives you the strength to continue pursuing goals. You will also find an evening reflection section where you can write what you accomplished today as well as what you are grateful for. Gratitude helps you appreciate the little and big things!

HEALTHY

Every Tuesday you will find a Self Care worksheet, with a gratitude section and a habit tracker - where you can track your water intake, how much you read, how many steps you took, how long you studied for. I am not sure of your specific need, so I left it blank for you to tailor this journal to your needs. You will also have a top three (3) list, related to the week's topic where you can reflect again and remind yourself of your priorities in life.

Spiritual

Every Wednesday, you will find a scriptural reflection. Growing up, Wednesday's were Bible study days for me. Having a relationship with the One who created you is so important and can help get you through the middle of the week or what society refers to as "hump day".

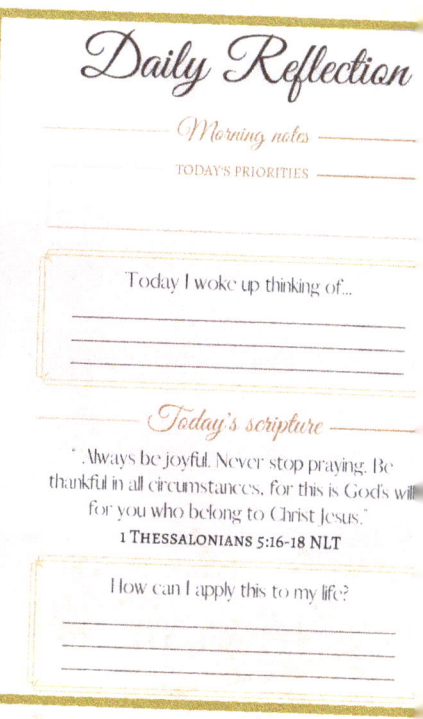

Write down your priorities and what you woke up thinking about, it will help clear your head and center your day. A scripture is included, reflect on how you can apply it do your daily life.

 # Goal Oriented

Each Saturday, you will find a progress worksheet that you can use to track and reflect on your accomplishments for the week and decide on how you can improve further.

PRACTICAL

For Thursdays, Fridays, and free days, I have included worksheets that pertain to weekly goals. Since the first week of the month is about gratitude and joy, finding and reflecting on what helps us deal best with stressors is important to ensure we have successful days, weeks, and months, which lead to prosperous years. The first week of the month is dedicated to establishing your priorities. Each first Thursday, I have provided a coping skills worksheet to help you identify what tools are best for you to apply in stressful situations.

Coping

Check the emotion
coping skills you lik

JOURNAL	( )	BREATHING
WRITE POETRY	( )	PICTURE A H
PLAY MUSIC	( )	COMPLIMENT
PRAY	( )	HANG OUT W
MAKE ART	( )	GO FISHING
COLOR	( )	READ A BOOK
TAKE A BATH	( )	WATCH A MO
DRINK TEA	( )	PLAY WITH A
GARDEN	( )	SPEND TIME
CLEAN AN AREA	( )	SEEK GODLY
COOK OR BAKE	( )	BEAUTY TREA
EXERCISE	( )	PLAY OR WAT
BIKE OR RUN	( )	MEDITATE O
DANCE	( )	GO FOR A WA

Establishing Priorities

I WANT	I NEED

HONEST

For the first Friday of each month, you will find a worksheet to help you establish your priorities. We have many wants in life, but everything that we want isn't always best for us, but maybe sometimes it is. Here you can write down your wants and then write down what you need.

POWERFUL

The second week of the month is dedicated as "the week to Purpose". You will find an affirmations worksheet for the 2nd Thursday of the month.

I encourage you to write out your affirmation or confessions. Write down what you are grateful for or what you want to see manifest in your life.

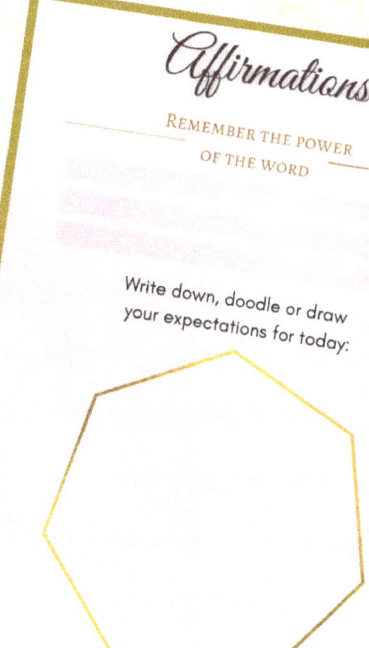

INTERACTIVE

The 2nd Friday of the month's activity sheet is dedicated to exploring you, where you are, what you have, and how you can use what you have to better understand, and finally fulfill your purpose in life.

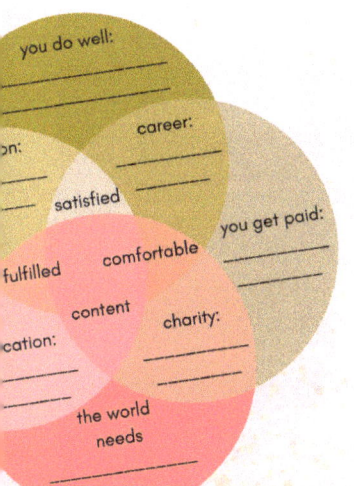

Brain Dump

WRITE/DRAW/EXPRESS YOURSELF TO RELEASE THE FEELINGS YOU DON'T WANT TO HOLD ON TO ANYMORE.

shame:

anger:

ANXIETY:

⇦ THERAPEUTIC

The third week of the month is dedicated to being open to new opportunities. Before you can embrace the new, you have to get rid of the old. So I dedicated the third Thursday of the month to releasing all our old and negative thoughts and emotions. I like to call this activity a Brain Dump.

Write down things you are ashamed of, angry about, or are anxious about. The Bible says in Romans 8: 1-2 KJV " There is therefore now no condemnation to them which are in Christ Jesus, who walk not after the flesh, but after the Spirit. For the law of the Spirit of life in Christ Jesus hath made me free from the law of sin and death." Write down those negative feelings, release them.

ACTIONABLE ⇨

It's only right that the 3rd Friday of the month should be dedicated to releasing negative thoughts and replacing them with positive ones. For example, if you feel " I am ugly." Replace that with a positive truth. " I am beautiful. I am fearfully and wonderfully made."

Replace

OLD BELIEFS	NEW

COMPLETE

Last but not least, the last week of each month is dedicated to embracing how powerful you are. Reflect on your month's journey by doing a simple but powerful "about me" assessment. Write down your vision and make it plain. Write down your dream life and your long term goals to accomplish that. Write down the lessons you have learned over the past month and what your strengths are. Write down what you found challenging, pray about it, and move on.

IMPORTANT

Then for the last Friday of each month, I have provided you with a personal growth reflections worksheet. Write down the area of your life that you are reflecting on such as parenting. Write down what you are doing well at such as cooking dinner etc. and then, write down things you can improve on such as yelling less while trying to get your son to stop yelling.

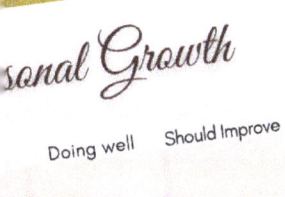

Rising to Purpose

What's your Big Why?

- Think about why you get up in the morning.
- Think about what you do best.
- Think about what makes you most happy.
- Now think about your dreams and how achievable they are.

Before you discover your whats and hows, you must identify your whys — your deep, personal motivation. (For example, maybe you want a big house for your kids, maybe it's freedom.) Whatever it is you must figure out your Why before figuring out your goal and how you'll achieve it.

USE THESE LINES TO WRITE OR DRAW YOUR BIG WHY.

Vision Board

Weekly Reflection

"ENJOY THE LITTLE THINGS, FOR ONE DAY YOU MAY LOOK BACK AND REALIZE THEY WERE THE BIG THINGS."
Robert Brault

Reflect on something you took for granted as a child but now have more of an appreciation for.

_____
_____
_____
_____
_____
_____

Weekly Goal

Start Date: _____

Achieve by: _____

Goal Description:
_____
_____
_____

Motivation:
_____
_____
_____

ACTIONABLE STEPS

- ○ _____
- ○ _____
- ○ _____
- ○ _____
- ○ _____
- ○ _____
- ○ _____
- ○ _____

My feelings about this goal...

_____
_____
_____
_____
_____
_____
_____

Daily Journal

Morning notes

TODAY'S MANTRA

Today I am looking forward to...

_____
_____
_____

Evening Reflections

TODAY I ACCOMPLISHED

Today I am grateful for...

_____
_____
_____

Self Care

―― TODAY'S GRATITUDE ――

Habit Tracker

☐☐☐☐☐☐☐ ☐☐☐☐☐☐☐

☐☐☐☐☐☐☐ ☐☐☐☐☐☐☐

☐☐☐☐☐☐☐ ☐☐☐☐☐☐☐

☐☐☐☐☐☐☐ ☐☐☐☐☐☐☐

Write down 3 simple pleasures you have in life:
1. _____
2. _____
3. _____

Daily Reflection

Morning notes

TODAY'S PRIORITIES

Today I woke up thinking of...

___

Today's scripture

" Always be joyful. Never stop praying. Be thankful in all circumstances, for this is God's will for you who belong to Christ Jesus."

1 Thessalonians 5:16-18 NLT

How can I apply this to my life?

___

Coping Skills

Check the emotion-based coping skills you like to do

Journal	( )	Breathing exercises	( )
Write poetry	( )	Picture a happy place	( )
Play music	( )	Compliment yourself	( )
Pray	( )	Hang out with friends	( )
Make art	( )	Go fishing	( )
Color	( )	Read a book	( )
Take a bath	( )	Watch a movie or show	( )
Drink tea	( )	Play with a pet	( )
Garden	( )	Spend time in nature	( )
Clean an area	( )	Seek godly advice	( )
Cook or bake	( )	Beauty treatments	( )
Exercise	( )	Play or watch sports	( )
Bike or Run	( )	Meditate on scripture	( )
Dance	( )	Go for a walk	( )

Establishing Priorities

I WANT I NEED

Progress Check

You started at:
_____

You will achieve by:
_____

Expectation X Reality:
_____
_____
_____

What are you learning?
_____
_____
_____

ACTIONABLE STEPS

- ◯
- ◯
- ◯
- ◯

- ◯
- ◯
- ◯
- ◯

My feelings about this goal...

_____
_____
_____
_____
_____
_____
_____

Weekly Reflection

"The two most important days of your life are the day you were born and the day you find out why."
Mark Twain

What is your Purpose? What is something you feel deeply that you were made to do in this world?

_____
_____
_____
_____
_____
_____
_____

Weekly Goal

Start Date: _____

Achieve by: _____

Goal Description:
_____
_____
_____

Motivation:
_____
_____
_____

ACTIONABLE STEPS

- ○ _____
- ○ _____
- ○ _____
- ○ _____
- ○ _____
- ○ _____
- ○ _____

My feelings about this goal...

_____
_____
_____
_____
_____
_____
_____

Daily Journal

Morning notes

TODAY'S MANTRA

Today I am looking forward to...

___

___

___

Evening Reflections

TODAY I ACCOMPLISHED

Today I am grateful for...

___

___

___

Self Care

TODAY'S GRATITUDE

Habit Tracker

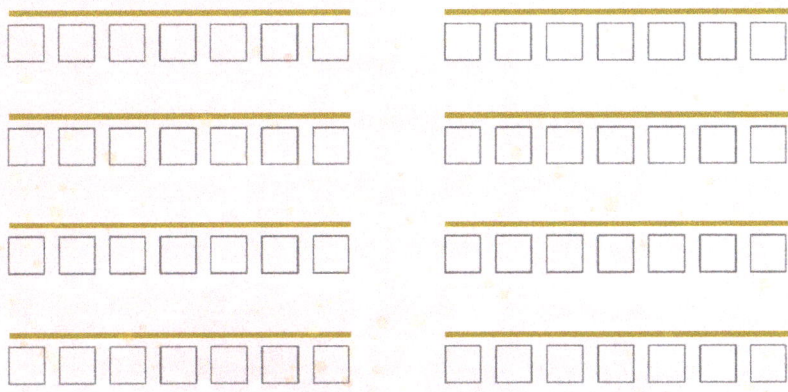

Write down 3 ways to fulfill your purpose today:

1. _____
2. _____
3. _____

Daily Reflection

Morning notes

TODAY'S PRIORITIES

Today I woke up thinking of...

Today's scripture

" For I know the plans I have for you," declares the LORD, " plans to prosper you and not to harm you, plans to give you hope and a future."

JEREMIAH 29:11 NIV

How can I apply this to my life?

Affirmations

Remember the power of the word

Write down, doodle or draw your expectations for today:

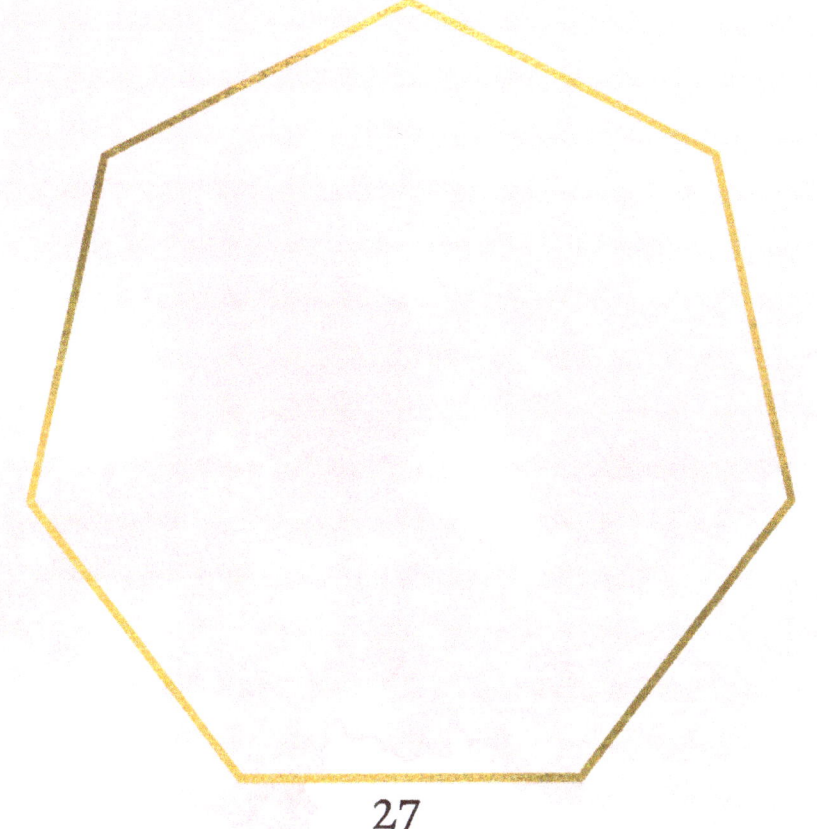

Find your purpose

PLEASE FILL IN WITH INFORMATION ABOUT YOU TO FIND YOUR PURPOSE!

you do well:
_____
_____

passion:
_____
_____

career:
_____
_____

satisfied

you love to do:
_____
_____

fulfilled   comfortable

you get paid:
_____
_____

content

vocation:
_____
_____

charity:
_____
_____

the world needs
_____
_____

Progress Check

You started at:
_____

You will achieve by:
_____

Expectation X Reality:
_____
_____
_____

What are you learning?
_____
_____
_____

ACTIONABLE STEPS

○ _____
○ _____
○ _____
○ _____

○ _____
○ _____
○ _____
○ _____

My feelings about this goal...

_____
_____
_____
_____
_____
_____
_____

Weekly Reflection

"Nobody can go back and start a new beginning, but anyone can start today and make a new ending."
Maria Robinson

How can you make room for a change in your life? What area of your life is in need of a brand new start?

_____
_____
_____
_____
_____
_____
_____

Weekly Goal

Start Date: _____

Achieve by: _____

Goal Description:
_____
_____
_____

Motivation:
_____
_____
_____

ACTIONABLE STEPS

- ○ _____
- ○ _____
- ○ _____
- ○ _____
- ○ _____
- ○ _____
- ○ _____
- ○ _____

My feelings about this goal...

_____
_____
_____
_____
_____
_____
_____
_____

Daily Journal

Morning notes

TODAY'S MANTRA

Today I am looking forward to...

_____

_____

Evening Reflections

TODAY I ACCOMPLISHED

Today I am grateful for...

_____

_____

Self Care

TODAY'S GRATITUDE

Habit Tracker

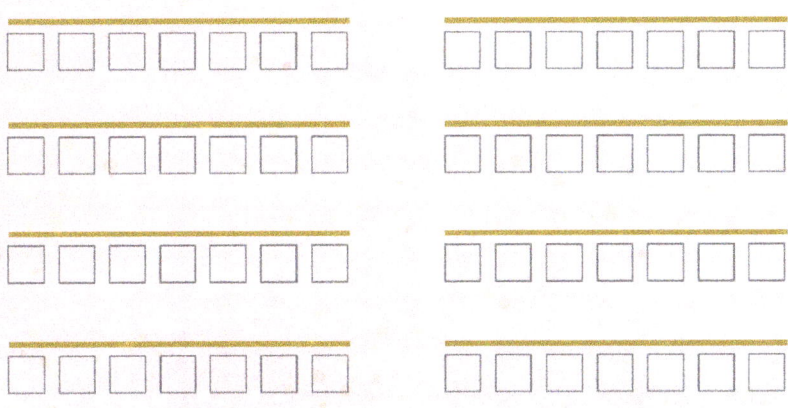

Write down 3 new beginnings you need to have:

1. _____
2. _____
3. _____

Daily Reflection

Morning notes

TODAY'S PRIORITIES

Today I woke up thinking of...

Today's scripture

" " But forget all that— it is nothing compared to what I am going to do. For I am about to do something new. See, I have already begun! Do you not see it? I will make a pathway through the wilderness. I will create rivers in the dry wasteland.

ISAIAH 43:18-19 NLT

How can I apply this to my life?

Brain Dump

Write/draw/express yourself to release the feelings you don't want to hold on to anymore.

shame:

anger:

ANXIETY:

Replace

OLD BELIEFS	NEW TRUTHS

Progress Check

You started at:
_____

You will achieve by:
_____

Expectation X Reality:
_____
_____
_____

What are you learning?
_____
_____
_____

ACTIONABLE STEPS

- ○ _____
- ○ _____
- ○ _____
- ○ _____

- ○ _____
- ○ _____
- ○ _____
- ○ _____

My feelings about this goal...

_____
_____
_____
_____
_____
_____
_____

Weekly Reflection

"TRUE HAPPINESS INVOLVES THE FULL USE OF ONE'S POWER AND TALENTS."
John W. Gardner

What is your superpower? What are your talents? How can you improve and make use of your full potential?

_____
_____
_____
_____
_____
_____
_____

Weekly Goal

Start Date: _____

Achieve by: _____

Goal Description:
_____
_____
_____

Motivation:
_____
_____
_____

Actionable Steps

- ○
- ○
- ○
- ○

- ○
- ○
- ○
- ○

My feelings about this goal...

_____
_____
_____
_____
_____
_____
_____

Daily Journal

Morning notes

TODAY'S MANTRA

Today I am looking forward to...

_____
_____
_____

Evening Reflections

TODAY I ACCOMPLISHED

Today I am grateful for...

_____
_____
_____

Self Care

TODAY'S GRATITUDE

Habit Tracker

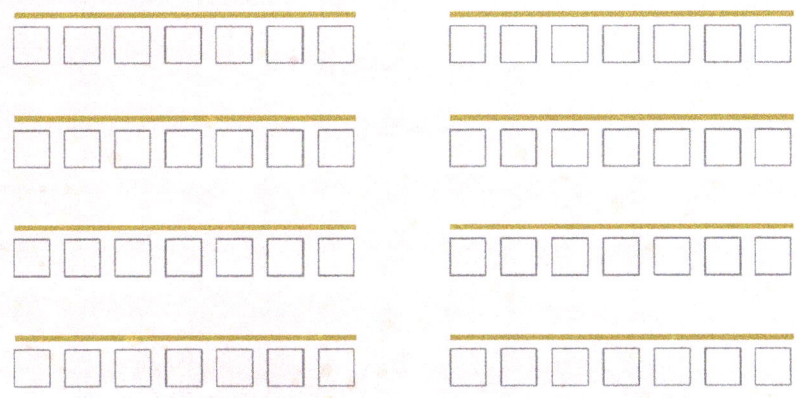

Write down 3 of your talents::

1. _____
2. _____
3. _____

Daily Reflection

Morning notes

TODAY'S PRIORITIES

Today I woke up thinking of...

Today's scripture

" I can do all things through Christ who strengthens me."

PHILIPPIANS 4:13 NKJV

How can I apply this to my life?

About Me

DREAM LIFE

LONG-TERM GOALS

LESSONS LEARNED

MY STRENGTHS

CHALLENGES

PRAY & MOVE ON

Personal Growth

Area of Life	Doing well	Should Improve

Progress Check

You started at:
_____

You will achieve by:
_____

Expectation X Reality:
_____
_____
_____

What are you learning?
_____
_____
_____

ACTIONABLE STEPS

- ○ _____
- ○ _____
- ○ _____
- ○ _____

- ○ _____
- ○ _____
- ○ _____
- ○ _____

My feelings about this goal...

_____
_____
_____
_____
_____
_____
_____

Notes

Notes

Weekly Reflection

"To speak gratitude is courteous and pleasant, to enact gratitude is generous and noble, but to live gratitude is to touch Heaven."
Johannes A. Gaertner

How can you show more appreciation and gratitude towards the people you love, like acknowledging their love?

_____
_____
_____
_____
_____
_____

Weekly Goal

Start Date: _____

Achieve by: _____

Goal Description:
_____
_____
_____

Motivation:
_____
_____
_____

ACTIONABLE STEPS

- ☐ _____
- ☐ _____
- ☐ _____
- ☐ _____

- ☐ _____
- ☐ _____
- ☐ _____
- ☐ _____

My feelings about this goal…

_____
_____
_____
_____
_____
_____
_____

Daily Journal

Morning notes

TODAY'S MANTRA

Today I am looking forward to...

_____

_____

Evening Reflections

TODAY I ACCOMPLISHED

Today I am grateful for...

_____

_____

Self Care

TODAY'S GRATITUDE

Habit Tracker

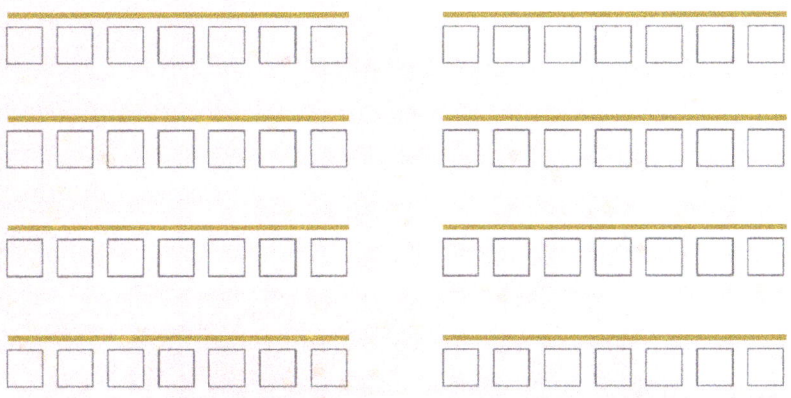

Write down 3 people you are grateful for:

1. _____
2. _____
3. _____

Daily Reflection

Morning notes

TODAY'S PRIORITIES

Today I woke up thinking of...

_____
_____
_____

Today's scripture

This is the day the LORD has made.
We will rejoice and be glad in it.
PSALMS 118: 24 NLT

How can I apply this to my life?

_____
_____
_____

Coping Skills

Check the emotion-based coping skills you like to do

Journal	( )	Breathing exercises	( )
Write poetry	( )	Picture a happy place	( )
Play music	( )	Compliment yourself	( )
Pray	( )	Hang out with friends	( )
Make art	( )	Go fishing	( )
Color	( )	Read a book	( )
Take a bath	( )	Watch a movie or show	( )
Drink tea	( )	Play with a pet	( )
Garden	( )	Spend time in nature	( )
Clean an area	( )	Seek godly advice	( )
Cook or bake	( )	Beauty treatments	( )
Exercise	( )	Play or watch sports	( )
Bike or Run	( )	Meditate on scripture	( )
Dance	( )	Go for a walk	( )

Establishing Priorities

I WANT	I NEED

Progress Check

You started at:
_____

You will achieve by:
_____

Expectation X Reality:
_____
_____
_____

What are you learning?
_____
_____
_____

ACTIONABLE STEPS

- ☐ _____
- ☐ _____
- ☐ _____
- ☐ _____

- ☐ _____
- ☐ _____
- ☐ _____
- ☐ _____

My feelings about this goal...

_____
_____
_____
_____
_____
_____
_____

Weekly Reflection

"It's not enough to have lived.
We should be determined
to live for something."
Winston S. Churchill

What are you living for? What is the deepest meaning behind your actions?

_____

_____

_____

_____

_____

_____

Weekly Goal

Start Date: _____

Achieve by: _____

Goal Description:
_____
_____
_____

Motivation:
_____
_____
_____

ACTIONABLE STEPS

- ○ _____
- ○ _____
- ○ _____
- ○ _____

- ○ _____
- ○ _____
- ○ _____
- ○ _____

My feelings about this goal...

_____
_____
_____
_____
_____
_____
_____

Daily Journal

Morning notes

TODAY'S MANTRA

Today I am looking forward to...

_____
_____
_____

Evening Reflections

TODAY I ACCOMPLISHED

Today I am grateful for...

_____
_____
_____

Self Care

TODAY'S GRATITUDE

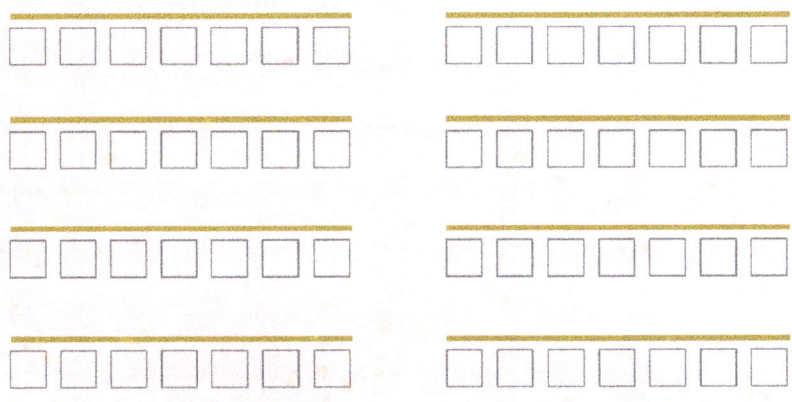

Habit Tracker

☐☐☐☐☐☐☐ ☐☐☐☐☐☐☐

☐☐☐☐☐☐☐ ☐☐☐☐☐☐☐

☐☐☐☐☐☐☐ ☐☐☐☐☐☐☐

☐☐☐☐☐☐☐ ☐☐☐☐☐☐☐

Write down 3 reasons you have to be alive:

1. _____
2. _____
3. _____

Daily Reflection

Morning notes

TODAY'S PRIORITIES

Today I woke up thinking of...

_____
_____
_____

Today's scripture

Many are the plans in a person's heart, but it is the LORD's purpose that prevails.

PROVERBS 19:21 NIV

How can I apply this to my life?

_____
_____
_____

Affirmations

REMEMBER THE POWER OF THE WORD

Write down, doodle or draw your expectations for today:

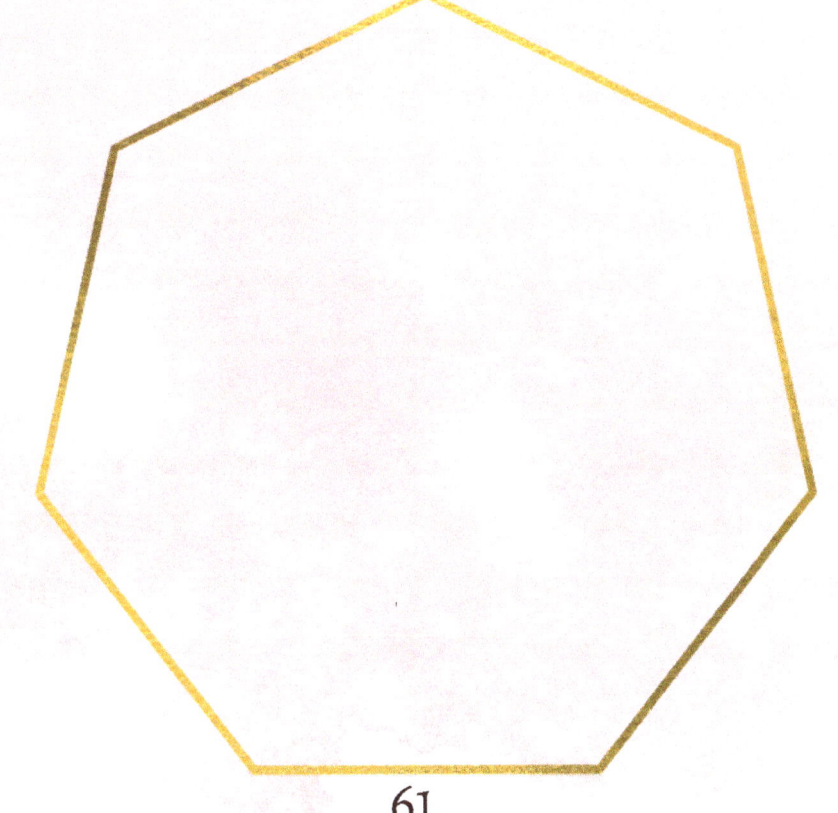

Find your purpose

PLEASE FILL IN WITH INFORMATION ABOUT YOU TO FIND YOUR PURPOSE!

you do well:
_____
_____

passion:
_____
_____

career:
_____
_____

satisfied

you love to do:
_____
_____

fulfilled   comfortable

content

vocation:
_____
_____

charity:
_____
_____

you get paid:
_____
_____

the world needs
_____
_____

Progress Check

You started at: | You will achieve by:
___

Expectation X Reality: | What are you learning?
___

ACTIONABLE STEPS

- ◯
- ◯
- ◯
- ◯

- ◯
- ◯
- ◯
- ◯

My feelings about this goal...

___

Weekly Reflection

"Nothing in the universe can stop you from letting go and starting over."

Guy Finley

What do you need to let go of? What in your life needs to be started over?

_____
_____
_____
_____
_____
_____

Weekly Goal

Start Date: _____

Achieve by: _____

Goal Description:
_____
_____
_____

Motivation:
_____
_____
_____

ACTIONABLE STEPS

- ○ _____
- ○ _____
- ○ _____
- ○ _____
- ○ _____
- ○ _____
- ○ _____
- ○ _____

My feelings about this goal...

_____
_____
_____
_____
_____
_____

Daily Journal

Morning notes

TODAY'S MANTRA

Today I am looking forward to...

_____
_____
_____

Evening Reflections

TODAY I ACCOMPLISHED

Today I am grateful for...

_____
_____
_____

Self Care

TODAY'S GRATITUDE

Habit Tracker

Write down 3 areas you need to start over:
1. _____
2. _____
3. _____

Daily Reflection

Morning notes

TODAY'S PRIORITIES

Today I woke up thinking of...

Today's scripture

This means that anyone who belongs to Christ
has become a new person. The old life
is gone; a new life has begun!

2 Corinthians 5:17 NLT

How can I apply this to my life?

Brain Dump

Write/draw/express yourself to release the feelings you don't want to hold on to anymore.

shame:

anger:

ANXIETY:

Replace

OLD BELIEFS	NEW TRUTHS

Progress Check

You started at:
_____

You will achieve by:
_____

Expectation X Reality:
_____
_____
_____

What are you learning?
_____
_____
_____

ACTIONABLE STEPS

- ○ _____
- ○ _____
- ○ _____
- ○ _____

- ○ _____
- ○ _____
- ○ _____

My feelings about this goal...

_____
_____
_____
_____
_____
_____
_____

Weekly Reflection

"THE POWER TO SHAPE YOUR REALITY LIES WITHIN YOU, THEREFORE THE MOST IMPORTANT VOICE YOU WILL EVER HEAR IS YOUR OWN."
Max Patrick

What can you tell yourself today that will uplift you to embrace your inner power? Acknowledge your capacities.

_____
_____
_____
_____
_____
_____

Weekly Goal

Start Date: _____

Achieve by: _____

Goal Description:
_____
_____
_____

Motivation:
_____
_____
_____

Actionable Steps

- ○ _____
- ○ _____
- ○ _____
- ○ _____
- ○ _____
- ○ _____
- ○ _____
- ○ _____

My feelings about this goal...

_____
_____
_____
_____
_____
_____
_____

Daily Journal

Morning notes

TODAY'S MANTRA

Today I am looking forward to...

_____
_____
_____

Evening Reflections

TODAY I ACCOMPLISHED

Today I am grateful for...

_____
_____
_____

Self Care

TODAY'S GRATITUDE

Habit Tracker

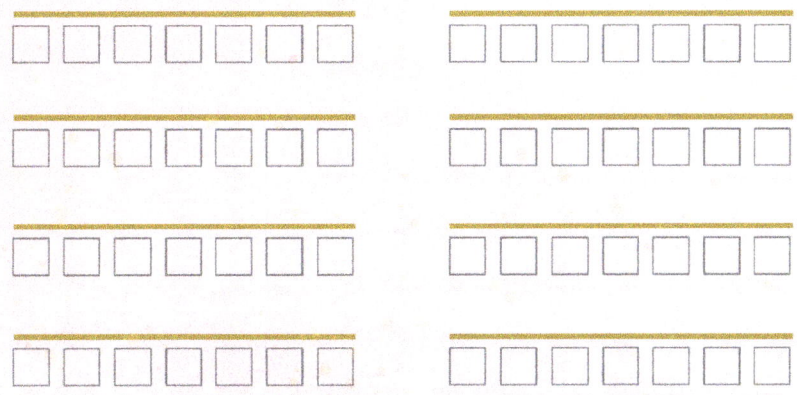

Write down 3 encouraging words to yourself::

1. _____
2. _____
3. _____

Daily Reflection

Morning notes

TODAY'S PRIORITIES

Today I woke up thinking of...
_____
_____
_____

Today's scripture

Be strong and courageous. Do not be afraid or terrified because of them, for the Lord your God goes with you; he will never leave you nor forsake you."

DEUTERONOMY 31:6 NIV

How can I apply this to my life?
_____
_____
_____

About Me

DREAM LIFE

LONG-TERM GOALS

LESSONS LEARNED

MY STRENGTHS

CHALLENGES

PRAY & MOVE ON

Personal Growth

Area of Life	Doing well	Should Improve

Progress Check

You started at:
_____

Expectation X Reality:
_____
_____
_____

You will achieve by:
_____

What are you learning?
_____
_____
_____

Actionable Steps

- ○ _____
- ○ _____
- ○ _____
- ○ _____
- ○ _____
- ○ _____
- ○ _____
- ○ _____

My feelings about this goal...

_____
_____
_____
_____
_____
_____

Notes

Notes

Weekly Reflection

"Gratitude turns what we have into enough, and more. It turns denial into acceptance, chaos into order, confusion into clarity... It makes sense of our past, brings peace for today, and creates a vision for tomorrow."

Melody Beattie

How do you feel when you give thanks? Write about the emotions you have when you are being grateful.

_____
_____
_____
_____
_____
_____

Weekly Goal

Start Date: _____

Achieve by: _____

Goal Description:
_____
_____
_____

Motivation:
_____
_____
_____

ACTIONABLE STEPS

- ○ _____
- ○ _____
- ○ _____
- ○ _____
- ○ _____
- ○ _____
- ○ _____
- ○ _____

My feelings about this goal...

_____
_____
_____
_____
_____
_____
_____
_____

Daily Journal

Morning notes

TODAY'S MANTRA

Today I am looking forward to...

_____
_____

Evening Reflections

TODAY I ACCOMPLISHED

Today I am grateful for...

_____
_____

Self Care

TODAY'S GRATITUDE

Habit Tracker

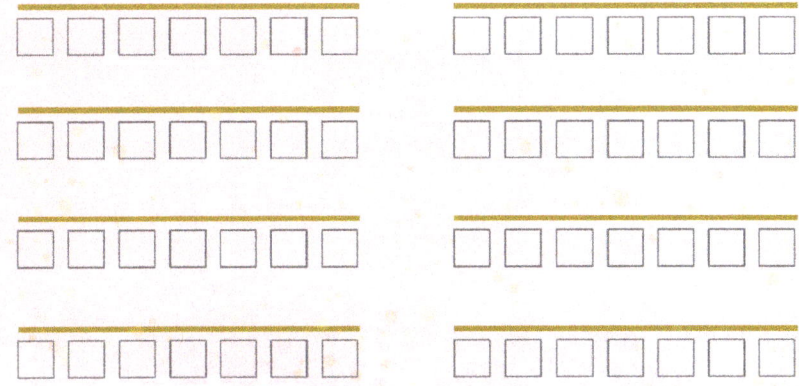

List 3 emotions that are associated with gratitude:

1. _____
2. _____
3. _____

Daily Reflection

Morning notes

TODAY'S PRIORITIES

Today I woke up thinking of...

_____
_____
_____

Today's scripture

And let the peace that comes from Christ rule in your hearts. For as members of one body you are called to live in peace. And always be thankful.

COLOSSIANS 3:15 NLT

How can I apply this to my life?

_____
_____
_____

Coping Skills

Check the emotion-based coping skills you like to do

Journal	( )	Breathing exercises	( )
Write poetry	( )	Picture a happy place	( )
Play music	( )	Compliment yourself	( )
Pray	( )	Hang out with friends	( )
Make art	( )	Go fishing	( )
Color	( )	Read a book	( )
Take a bath	( )	Watch a movie or show	( )
Drink tea	( )	Play with a pet	( )
Garden	( )	Spend time in nature	( )
Clean an area	( )	Seek godly advice	( )
Cook or bake	( )	Beauty treatments	( )
Exercise	( )	Play or watch sports	( )
Bike or Run	( )	Meditate on scripture	( )
Dance	( )	Go for a walk	( )

Establishing Priorities

I WANT	I NEED

Progress Check

You started at:
_____

You will achieve by:
_____

Expectation X Reality:
_____
_____
_____

What are you learning?
_____
_____
_____

ACTIONABLE STEPS

- ○ _____
- ○ _____
- ○ _____
- ○ _____

- ○ _____
- ○ _____
- ○ _____
- ○ _____

My feelings about this goal...

_____
_____
_____
_____
_____
_____
_____

Weekly Reflection

IF YOU CAN DREAM IT, YOU CAN DO IT.
Walt Disney

What is it that you want to achieve?
What is the purpose of this dream?

_____
_____
_____
_____
_____
_____
_____

Weekly Goal

Start Date: _____

Achieve by: _____

Goal Description:
_____
_____
_____

Motivation:
_____
_____
_____

ACTIONABLE STEPS

- ○ _____
- ○ _____
- ○ _____
- ○ _____
- ○ _____
- ○ _____
- ○ _____
- ○ _____

My feelings about this goal...

_____
_____
_____
_____
_____
_____

Daily Journal

Morning notes

TODAY'S MANTRA

Today I am looking forward to...

_____
_____

Evening Reflections

TODAY I ACCOMPLISHED

Today I am grateful for...

_____
_____

Self Care

TODAY'S GRATITUDE

Habit Tracker

☐☐☐☐☐☐☐ ☐☐☐☐☐☐☐

☐☐☐☐☐☐☐ ☐☐☐☐☐☐☐

☐☐☐☐☐☐☐ ☐☐☐☐☐☐☐

☐☐☐☐☐☐☐ ☐☐☐☐☐☐☐

Write down 3 goals related to your purpose:
1. _____
2. _____
3. _____

Daily Reflection

Morning notes

TODAY'S PRIORITIES

Today I woke up thinking of...

___

Today's scripture

"And we know that in all things God works for the good of those who love him, who have been called according to his purpose."
ROMANS 8:28 NIV

How can I apply this to my life?

___

Affirmations

Remember the power of the word

Write down, doodle or draw your expectations for today:

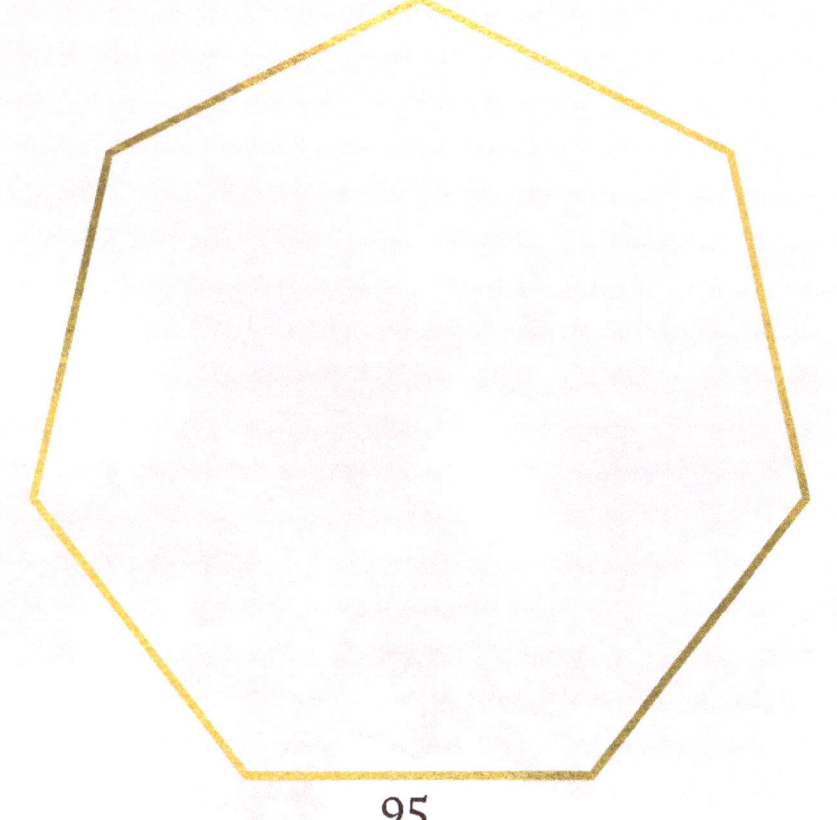

Find your purpose

PLEASE FILL IN WITH INFORMATION ABOUT YOU TO FIND YOUR PURPOSE!

you do well:
_____
_____

passion:
_____
_____

career:
_____
_____

satisfied

you love to do:
_____
_____

fulfilled

comfortable

you get paid:
_____
_____

content

vocation:
_____
_____

charity:
_____
_____

the world needs
_____
_____

Progress Check

You started at:
_____

You will achieve by:
_____

Expectation X Reality:
_____
_____
_____

What are you learning?
_____
_____
_____

ACTIONABLE STEPS

- ○ _____
- ○ _____
- ○ _____
- ○ _____

- ○ _____
- ○ _____
- ○ _____
- ○ _____

My feelings about this goal...

_____
_____
_____
_____
_____
_____
_____

Weekly Reflection

"Although no one can go back and make a brand new start, anyone can start from now and make a brand new beginning."
Carl Bard

Think of a fresh beginning you can have at this specific moment. What will you begin now?

_____
_____
_____
_____
_____
_____

Weekly Goal

Start Date: _____

Achieve by: _____

Goal Description:
_____
_____
_____

Motivation:
_____
_____
_____

ACTIONABLE STEPS

- ◯ _____
- ◯ _____
- ◯ _____
- ◯ _____

- ◯ _____
- ◯ _____
- ◯ _____

My feelings about this goal...

_____
_____
_____
_____
_____
_____
_____

Daily Journal

Morning notes

TODAY'S MANTRA

Today I am looking forward to...

_____
_____
_____

Evening Reflections

TODAY I ACCOMPLISHED

Today I am grateful for...

_____
_____
_____

Self Care

TODAY'S GRATITUDE

Habit Tracker

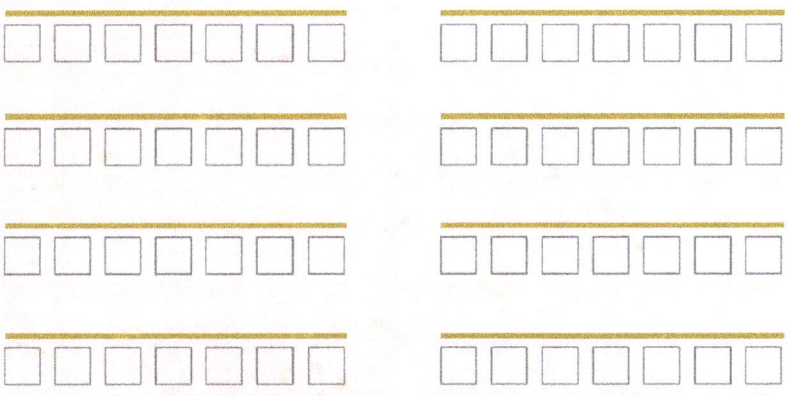

Write down 3 new beginnings you can have now:
1. _____
2. _____
3. _____

Daily Reflection

Morning notes

TODAY'S PRIORITIES

Today I woke up thinking of...

Today's scripture

"Your beginnings will seem humble, so prosperous will your future be."
Job 8:7 NIV

How can I apply this to my life?

Brain Dump

Write/draw/express yourself to release the feelings you don't want to hold on to anymore.

shame:

anger:

ANXIETY:

Replace

OLD BELIEFS	NEW TRUTHS

Progress Check

You started at:
_____

You will achieve by:
_____

Expectation X Reality:
_____
_____
_____

What are you learning?
_____
_____
_____

ACTIONABLE STEPS

- ○
- ○
- ○
- ○

- ○
- ○
- ○
- ○

My feelings about this goal...

_____
_____
_____
_____
_____
_____
_____

Weekly Reflection

"You do not need any more strength. You need only to realize how strong you already are."

Vironika Tugaleva

Remember a time where you were brave and strong to deal with something, and be thankful to yourself.

_____
_____
_____
_____
_____
_____
_____

Weekly Goal

Start Date: _____

Achieve by: _____

Goal Description:
_____
_____
_____

Motivation:
_____
_____
_____

ACTIONABLE STEPS

- ☐ _____
- ☐ _____
- ☐ _____
- ☐ _____

- ☐ _____
- ☐ _____
- ☐ _____
- ☐ _____

My feelings about this goal...

_____
_____
_____
_____
_____
_____
_____

Daily Journal

Morning notes

TODAY'S MANTRA

Today I am looking forward to...

_____
_____
_____

Evening Reflections

TODAY I ACCOMPLISHED

Today I am grateful for...

_____
_____
_____

Self Care

TODAY'S GRATITUDE

Habit Tracker

☐☐☐☐☐☐☐ ☐☐☐☐☐☐☐

☐☐☐☐☐☐☐ ☐☐☐☐☐☐☐

☐☐☐☐☐☐☐ ☐☐☐☐☐☐☐

☐☐☐☐☐☐☐ ☐☐☐☐☐☐☐

Write down 3 of your strengths:
1. _____
2. _____
3. _____

Daily Reflection

Morning notes

TODAY'S PRIORITIES

Today I woke up thinking of...

Today's scripture

"Have I not commanded you? Be strong and courageous. Do not be afraid; do not be discouraged, for the LORD your God will be with you wherever you go."

JOSHUA 1:9 NIV

How can I apply this to my life?

About Me

DREAM LIFE	LONG-TERM GOALS

LESSONS LEARNED	MY STRENGTHS

CHALLENGES	PRAY & MOVE ON

Personal Growth

Area of Life	Doing well	Should Improve

Progress Check

You started at:
_____

You will achieve by:
_____

Expectation X Reality:
_____
_____
_____

What are you learning?
_____
_____
_____

ACTIONABLE STEPS

- ○ _____
- ○ _____
- ○ _____
- ○ _____

- ○ _____
- ○ _____
- ○ _____
- ○ _____

My feelings about this goal...

_____
_____
_____
_____
_____
_____
_____

Notes

Notes

Conclusion

THANK YOU FOR OPENING YOUR HEART AND ENTERING THIS JOURNEY WITH ME.

You have finished this journal, but make a vow to yourself to continue practicing everything you learned here.

- How gratitude can impact your quality of life.
- How your purpose is so important and is what makes you unique in this world.
- Then take advantage of new possibilities every day and use every moment to keep improving.
- Acknowledge the power you have within you to make your dreams come true and bring your visions to life!

You have God on your side and if you see you how He sees you, you will build a brand new perspective of yourself and you will rise!
Go out and achieve your dreams, you will be victorious and prosperous.

Thank you for being amazing!

Join The Rising Family

For more inspiration and useful tips on reaching your purpose, visit the links below to connect with me on my website, or socials.

Also be sure to get your copy of my book:

Rise: A Collection of Inspiration Poetry, Prose and Affirmations.

https://www.shanadanielle.com/books

KEEP IN TOUCH WITH SHANA DANIELLE

Blog:
www.ShanaDanielle.com/Its-time-to-rise-blog

  @iamshanadanielle

 @imshanadanielle

www.ingramcontent.com/pod-product-compliance
Lightning Source LLC
Chambersburg PA
CBHW042116100526
44587CB00025B/4076